Here's the Pitch

James A. Lopez

Twi-Night Ink Press

March 23, 2001

Brendon,
Do you pitch to win, or do you pitch not to lose?

Have a great season,
Jim Lopez

Here's the Pitch. Copyright ©1998 by James A. Lopez. Printed and bound in Canada by Hemlock Printers Ltd. All rights reserved. No part of this book may be reproduced in any form or by any electronic or mechanical means including information storage and retrieval systems without permission in writing from the publisher, except by a reviewer who may quote brief passages in a review. Published by Twi-Night Ink Press, 950 Pacific Avenue, Suite 450, Tacoma, Washington 98402. (253)383-1964. (253)383-1808 fax. E-mail LLHlaw@aol.com

Articles on Steve Carlton and Mike Mussina reprinted by permission of *The News Tribune* (Tacoma, Washington).

Publisher's Cataloging-in-Publication
(Provided by Quality Books, Inc.)

Lopez, James A.
Here's the pitch / James A. Lopez. — 1st ed.
p. cm.
Preassigned LCCN: 98-90578
ISBN: 0-9666093-0-1

1. Pitching (Baseball) — Psychological aspects.
2. Baseball — Psychological aspects I. Title.

GV871.L66 1998   796.357'22
                        QBI98-951

Contents

Preface	5
Introduction	7
Instructions For Use Of This Work	7
FIRST INNING – *Introduction To Myself*	9
SECOND INNING – *Getting On The Mound And Staying There (Mind Over Matter?)*	45
It's All Matter To Me	45
What's In My Mind?	56
Speaking My Mind	66
Mixed Messages?	78
Nothing Matters If I Don't Mind	84
THIRD INNING – *My Team And My Coach*	109
My Team	109
My Coach	124
FOURTH INNING – *Game Day*	139
FIFTH INNING – *Having Fun And Playing Baseball*	157
SIXTH INNING – *Breathing Life Into Myself*	175
SEVENTH INNING – *Personal Evaluation*	179
EIGHTH INNING – *Why Am I Doing This?*	199
NINTH INNING – *Here's The Pitch – A Method*	205
The Dime	205
About The Author	208

"Simplify, simplify."

Henry David Thoreau

Preface

All too often in life, results are valued more than the person who brings about the results. The emphasis on results is not peculiar to baseball or sports in general. It is found virtually everywhere we go and in everything we do.

Where, in baseball, the landmark of civilization, do we find the humanistic spirit? How do we kindle it in our youth? How do we preserve it for all time? When will we learn that children, and adults, will have fun and perform better if they are educated, relaxed, and treated with dignity and respect? Coaches, and players, must treat each other with dignity and respect – after all, they are on the same team, aren't they? Sometimes, however, we wonder.

There are coaches who tell players to just get on the field and play. Pitchers, either child or adult, take the mound and are expected to get batters out. If they do, everything is fine. If they don't, what becomes of them?

Where in this process is there found an interest in the cultivation and nurturing of the pitcher as a person? His mental side – the most important side? The side that will make him an effective pitcher?

I wrote this book to give pitchers and coaches a starting point for understanding themselves and each other so that they truly will be on the same team. If a pitcher is expected to be effective – so must his coach. Pitchers and coaches will thrive in an environment that is conducive to learning and playing.

A pitcher, by nature, is a person long before he picks up a baseball. To become an effective pitcher is a life-long undertaking. Thus, if we pitchers take the time to find out who we are, what we are, and how and why we think and feel – when we step onto the mound we can battle the opposition rather than ourselves and our coaches. A pitcher can trust in only himself when he is on the mound.

I have been a person for forty-nine years. I first touched a baseball at the age of five and have played and/or coached since. Through the years, I have given pitching instruction to children as young as five and to adults over fifty. A pitcher is never too old to be effective.

The best coaches I have ever had are my parents, Sam and Helen Lopez. Without them, I would not be the person I am today. Thanks, Mom and Dad.

I also wish to thank my childhood baseball coach, Joe Rios, who, along with my Dad, made winners out of the kids and teams they coached. A special thanks to my first pitching coach, Carl Spahr, wherever he may be, for the meaningful and caring instruction he gave me.

Thanks go out to my brother, David Lopez, and Michelle Cox, for their tirelessly discussing life and baseball.

A special thanks to everyone in my law firm of Lowenberg, Lopez & Hansen, P.S. for their assistance in preparing this book for print. Thanks Debbie Holden for your technical and artistic assistance. Thanks Leann Kohten for keeping me semi-literate on the personal computer. Thanks Steve Hansen for your editing efforts. Thanks Tim Lowenberg for always finding baseball shirts for me with great motivational language on them.

I am especially grateful to my designer, Paul Langland, for his very professional efforts in preparing this book for printing.

A greatly appreciative thanks to my friends and teammates, Dave Mathews and Mic Stump, for all the games we have played together and for our discussions.

My very special thanks to my favorite Lynda Ross for her love, enthusiasm, and support. Without her, this project could not have been completed.

The proper mechanics of pitching a baseball are clear. Every pitcher, however, is different in mental makeup. This is why no pitcher is a carbon copy, or should be referred to as such, of another pitcher. If a pitcher is determined, ingenious, and methodical, he will become an effective pitcher.

James A. Lopez
Tacoma, Washington
May 12, 1998

Introduction

The mental aspects of pitching are crucial and provide the foundation for you as a person and as a pitcher. This work is intended to be utilized by you in conjunction with good coaching on technique, fitness, and nutrition. But, at this juncture, let us explore your mental side so that you will be in the right frame of mind when you take the mound.

Instructions for Use of this Work

Use this work as an analytical tool and memoir for the rest of your pitching life. Your succinct answers should be dated and written in the spaces provided. Through the years, you will need to add answer sheets in order to accurately record your insight and development.

For any questions that require a written answer other than a yes or no, please be brief and organized. Portions of this work do not require an answer, however, please keep your response short if you wish to comment on the point.

As soon as you receive this work, complete one chapter each day for the next nine days. Study each chapter well and remember the questions or points to assist you in your periodic review of the areas in which you need to work, improve, or further understand.

Use this work during both the good and the not-so-good times you experience as a pitcher. Always accentuate the positive on your journey toward becoming an effective pitcher. After all – without having the mental aspects of pitching under control, sheer physical ability will not carry the day for you.

You will notice that your answers may be different due to your particular mental state at the time you review portions of this work. Your goal is to have consistent, complete, well-understood, and fully developed mental principles as a pitcher. Optimally, your reference to this work may become less and less as your consciousness increases.

If you are using this work under the guidance of a pitching coach, you will answer the questions and return the book to your coach. The coach will review your answers and return the book to you as often as necessary and call your attention to certain questions or chapters upon which you need to focus. You will date and answer the specific questions and return the book to your coach. The following day your coach will review your answers in a one-on-one session. Your coach can also ask follow-up questions by dating and writing them in the book and returning it to you for response.

In the event you are not using this work under the guidance of a pitching coach, then treat yourself as both the pitcher and the coach. Let your good conscience and your intellectual and personal honesty be your constant companions. Remember, you are on your own when you take the mound. Trust yourself. Rely upon yourself.

Your answers are always confidential. Please give serious thought to each question before you answer. It is important that you periodically review and ask yourself the questions in this book.

If you do not know or are uncertain of the meaning of any words in this work, please go the distance and look them up in the dictionary. It is important that we do not get our signals crossed.

Do not look into the questions to try and find the "right" answer. Look into yourself for the answer. Learning, and understanding, are for you in life – not for your parents, your friends, your coach, or this author. Relax and have fun!

First Inning

Introduction To Myself

QUESTION: Do I want to turn to the next page?

Date	Answer

QUESTION: Why did I want to turn to this page?

Date	Answer

QUESTION: Do I want to live my life the same way I answered the previous question?

Date	Answer

QUESTION: Do I love life?

Date	Answer

QUESTION: Do I love myself?

Date	Answer

QUESTION: Do I love baseball?

Date	Answer

QUESTION: Why do I love baseball?

Date	Answer

QUESTION: Do I believe I should have fun when I play baseball?

Date	Answer

QUESTION: Do I believe I should relax when I play baseball?

Date	Answer

QUESTION: Do I believe I should work hard when I play baseball?

Date	Answer

QUESTION: Do I believe I should work effectively when I play baseball?

Date	Answer

QUESTION: What is the difference, if any, between working hard and working effectively when I play baseball?

Date	Answer

QUESTION: Do I have faith in myself as a person?

Date	Answer

QUESTION: Do I have faith in myself as a pitcher?

Date	Answer

QUESTION: Do I have faith that things will always work out no matter what?

Date	Answer

QUESTION: Should I have faith in myself even if I am not a regular starting or relief pitcher?

Date	Answer

QUESTION: Why should I have faith in myself even if I am not a regular starting or relief pitcher?

Date	Answer

QUESTION: Do I sometimes not try as hard as I should when I am playing baseball?

Date	Answer

QUESTION: Do I know that I should always try to do my best no matter what?

Date	Answer

QUESTION: Does this mean I should try hard to do my best in practice and in games?

Date	Answer

QUESTION: Do I plan to do my best in life no matter what?

Date	Answer

QUESTION: Do I want to learn to become a pitcher?

Date	Answer

QUESTION: Am I willing to listen in order to become a pitcher?

Date	Answer

QUESTION: Do I believe that there is something to learn in everything I see, hear, or do?

Date	Answer

QUESTION: Am I willing to be receptive to change in order to become an effective pitcher?

Date	Answer

QUESTION: Am I willing to ask questions in order to become an effective pitcher?

Date	Answer

QUESTION: For the previous questions, please place the number of the "yes" answers and the "no" answers to those questions in the space below.

Date	Answer

QUESTION: Were all of my answers to those questions a "yes" answer? What does this mean to me?

Date	Answer

QUESTION: If any of my answers to the questions were "no," please explain each "no" answer below.

Date	Answer

QUESTION: Were any of my answers to the previous questions other than a "yes" or a "no?" If so, please explain for each answer that was other than a "yes" or a "no."

Date	Answer

QUESTION: Upon whom, then, does my completeness as a person depend?

Date	Answer

QUESTION: Upon whom, then, does my completeness as a pitcher depend?

Date	Answer

QUESTION: Anybody else?

Date	Answer

QUESTION: Am I determined to become an effective pitcher?

Date	Answer

Mental Perspective

DETERMINATION

According to Webster's Third New International Dictionary (1993), determination is defined as ". . . the act of deciding definitely and firmly . . . the power or habit of deciding definitely and firmly . . . [the] ability to persist against opposition or attempts to dissuade or discourage."

I love this game and nothing is going to stand in the way of my playing it. In order to become an effective pitcher, I must be determined. I shall be determined forever!

Notes To Myself

SECOND INNING

*Getting On The Mound And Staying There
(Mind Over Matter?)
It's All Matter To Me*

QUESTION: Am I in excellent physical condition?

Date	Answer

QUESTION: Am I able to consistently spot my fastball to any location?

Date	Answer

QUESTION: Am I able to vary the speed of my fastball to give at least three speeds?

Date	Answer

QUESTION: Am I able to consistently spot my curve to any location?

Date	Answer

QUESTION: Am I able to vary the speed of my curve to give at least three speeds?

Date	Answer

QUESTION: Am I able to throw my changeup or other specialty pitch to any location on command?

Date	Answer

QUESTION: Am I able to throw any other of my specialty pitches to any location and with varying speeds?

Date	Answer

QUESTION: Am I able to field my position as a pitcher effectively?

Date	Answer

QUESTION: Am I able to throw accurately to any bag on a pick-off play and pick-off base runners?

Date	Answer

QUESTION: Do I know how to warm up properly and have I warmed up properly before each game?

Date	Answer

QUESTION: Am I able to breathe correctly?

Date	Answer

What's In My Mind?

QUESTION: Am I willing to think while I am pitching?

Date	Answer

QUESTION: Am I willing to feel while I am pitching?

Date	Answer

Question: What balance, if any, should there be between thinking and feeling while I am pitching?

Date	Answer

QUESTION: Am I willing to try to understand my emotions?

Date	Answer

QUESTION: Am I willing to control my emotions?

Date	Answer

QUESTION: Should I control my emotions?

Date	Answer

QUESTION: Do I ever suffer from anxiety before, during, or after a game?

Date	Answer

QUESTION: How do I deal with this anxiety?

Date	Answer

QUESTION: Is anxiety an emotion with which I must deal in order to become a pitcher?

Date	Answer

QUESTION: What is my plan to deal with anxiety?

Date	Answer

Speaking My Mind

In order to answer this question, I must be home and have access to a mirror. There should be nobody else in the room during this exercise.

Look into the mirror and say to the batter: "You are going to have to hit me!"

QUESTION: How convinced was I of what I said to the batter in the previous question?

Date	Answer

*Look into the mirror and say to the batter:
"You are going to have to hit me!"*

QUESTION: How convinced was I of what I said to the batter this time?

Date	Answer

*Look into the mirror and say to the batter:
"You are going to have to hit me!"*

QUESTION: How convinced was I this time?

Date	Answer

Question: What am I learning by being asked the same question three times?

Date	Answer

Same scenario. Look into the mirror, the batter is in the box, and say to the batter: "I'm going to get you out!"

QUESTION: Was I convinced by what I said?

Date	Answer

QUESTION: Why was I convinced or not convinced?

Date	Answer

QUESTION: Therefore, how can I transform what I say into what I do?

Date	Answer

Mental Perspective

Reduce Everything To Its Elements

Steve Carlton is a four-time Cy Young award winner and is a member of the Baseball Hall of Fame. His lifetime record is 329-243. His lifetime earned run average is 3.19. Steve Carlton pitched 23 years in the majors.

While playing for the Philadelphia Phillies in 1980, he pitched against the Kansas City Royals in the World Series. He was 2 and 0 with a 2.40 earned run average.

With respect to the 1980 World Series, and Steve Carlton's remembrance of George Brett and the Kansas City Royals:

> *"I didn't see Brett," he said. "I didn't notice they were on the field. To me, it was another game of catch."*

Mixed Messages?

QUESTION: Do I believe that there is a different thought and feeling process between a starting pitcher and a relief pitcher?

Date	Answer

QUESTION: If I believe that there is a different thought and feeling process between a starting pitcher and a relief pitcher, please describe.

Date	Answer

QUESTION: If I believe that there is a difference between the thought and feeling process of a starter and reliever, which thought and feeling process do I prefer?

Date	Answer

QUESTION: In order to fulfill the pitching role of both a starter and a reliever, what must I do physically and mentally?

Date	Answer

QUESTION: Why should there be a different thought and feeling process between a starting pitcher and a relief pitcher?

Date	Answer

Mental Perspective

Regardless of my belief as to whether there exists a different thought and feeling process between a starting pitcher and a relief pitcher, or the role in which the coach may place me, remember:

- I know that the game is on the line from the first batter to the last batter.

- Be tenacious at all times whether I am going nine innings or nine pitches.

- I know that I am going to get outs no matter how long it takes.

- My duty as a pitcher is to get batters out and there are no exceptions. Thus, how can I justify a different mind-set depending upon whether I am a starter or a reliever?

- I avoid labeling myself as a starter or a reliever because if I so confine myself, I may not achieve my maximum potential.

- The luxury of having the same mind-set of a starter and a reliever is that I will always know how to respond in the role of each. I will always think outside the box so that I will never find myself inside the box.

Nothing Matters If I Don't Mind

Question: I am on the mound and the second baseman makes an error on a play that allows the runner to reach base safely. How, typically, would I think and feel about this occurrence?

Date	Answer

QUESTION: The scenario is the same as the previous page, however, the second baseman makes another error on the next batter. How, typically, would I think and feel about this second error by the same player?

Date	Answer

QUESTION: Same scenario as the previous two questions, except that the third batter I pitch to reaches base safely because of an error by the left fielder thereby loading the bases. How, typically, would I think and feel about this occurrence?

Date	Answer

QUESTION: Same scenario as the previous three questions, except that with the bases loaded the batter hits the ball in front of home plate, the catcher fields the ball and throws it over the first baseman's head and three runners score. How, typically, would I think and feel about this?

Date	Answer

QUESTION: I have thrown three straight balls to the batter. The count is 3-and-0. What is on my mind?

Date	Answer

QUESTION: What am I going to do about this 3-and-0 count?

Date	Answer

QUESTION: How am I going to accomplish my goal on this batter with a 3-and-0 count?

Date	Answer

QUESTION: Would my answer to the last three questions be any different if the bases were empty or the bases were loaded?

Date	Answer

QUESTION: I am on the mound and waiting for the next batter to step into the box. I hear the batter's teammate in the on-deck circle say to the batter: "This pitcher can't get anything over the plate. Here's an easy on-base for you." What do I think and feel?

Date	Answer

QUESTION: I am on the mound. A batter is getting ready to step into the box. Someone in the stands says to the batter in the box: "Rope him for a triple like the last two batters did." What do I think and feel?

Date	Answer

QUESTION: I am on the mound, the batter steps into the box, and I can hear one of my teammates on the bench saying: "Hope he doesn't give up another bomb." What do I think and feel?

Date	Answer

QUESTION: I am on the mound, the batter steps into the box, and I hear my coach saying about me: "My own pitcher can't get anything over the plate." What do I think and feel?

Date	Answer

QUESTION: I am on the mound and the batter steps into the box. The third base coach says to the batter: "C'mon, hit that beach ball!" What do I think and feel?

Date	Answer

Question: How should I think and feel about the scenarios set forth in the previous questions?

Date	Answer

QUESTION: It is the top of the first inning, I am on the mound, I am on the rubber to take the sign, and the catcher calls for a changeup. What is the first thought that enters my mind?

Date	Answer

QUESTION: It is the top of the first inning, I am on the mound, I am on the rubber to take the sign, and the catcher calls for a knuckleball or another of my specialty pitches. What is the first thought that enters my mind?

Date	Answer

QUESTION: It is the top of the first inning, I am on the mound, I am on the rubber to take the sign, and the catcher calls for a fastball. What is the first thought that enters my mind?

Date	Answer

QUESTION: It is the top of the first inning, I am on the mound, I am on the rubber to take the sign, and the catcher calls for a curveball. What is the first thought that enters my mind?

Date	Answer

QUESTION: It is the top of the first inning, I am on the mound, I am on the rubber to take the sign, and the catcher calls for a slider. What is the first thought that enters my mind?

Date	Answer

QUESTION: How should I respond to all five of the above scenarios?

Date	Answer

QUESTION: I have received the sign from the catcher. I throw the first pitch. It is a monster home run. What am I thinking and feeling?

Date	Answer

QUESTION: How should I think and feel?

Date	Answer

QUESTION: I am having a great year on the mound and my earned run average is under 2.00. My record is 6 and 0. I have just pitched a 2 hit shutout. The next game I pitch, I walk 7 batters in three innings, give up 9 earned runs, and am taken out of the game in the third inning. How, typically, would I think and feel about myself as a pitcher?

Date	Answer

Mental Perspective

Ingenuity

Ingenious

According to Webster's Third New International Dictionary (1993), ingenious is defined as "... marked by originality, resourcefulness, and cleverness in conception or execution ..."

I love this game and nothing is going to stand in the way of my playing it. There are no limits to what is in my mind!

Mussina Kept Mariners Guessing

Orioles starter Mike Mussina had it all working Sunday. He threw five pitches consistently for strikes: a fastball, a curve, a slider, a changeup and a cut fastball.

His strikeout of Edgar Martinez in the sixth inning, after falling behind 3-and-0, offers an example of the command Mussina had.

"You can't just sit on one pitch with him, and that makes it very difficult, especially because of the way he changes pitches," Martinez said. "He threw two breaking pitches to me with a 3-1 count, and I couldn't believe it."

Referring to Martinez's at-bat, Ray Miller, the Orioles' pitching coach said: "We've got a two-run lead and the count is 3-1, and Moose nails a couple of curveballs. You look over at the other team in the dugout, and they're saying, 'Holy smokes.'"

Notes To Myself

Third Inning

My Team And My Coach
My Team

QUESTION: Do I believe I have something to contribute to my team?

Date	Answer

QUESTION: What do I believe I have to contribute to my team?

Date	Answer

QUESTION: Do I believe that every person on the team has something to contribute to the team?

Date	Answer

QUESTION: Do I believe that I am less important to the team if I am not considered to be one of the best pitchers on the team?

Date	Answer

QUESTION: Have I ever felt that I was not an important part of the team?

Date	Answer

QUESTION: When did I feel that I was not an important part of the team?

Date	Answer

QUESTION: Why did I feel that I was not an important part of the team?

Date	Answer

QUESTION: What did I do about my feeling that I was not an important part of the team?

Date	Answer

QUESTION: What should I have done about my feeling that I was not an important part of the team?

Date	Answer

QUESTION: How should I feel about my importance to the team?

Date	Answer

QUESTION: Do I believe I am a unique human being?

Date	Answer

QUESTION: Do I believe I am different than all other pitchers?

Date	Answer

QUESTION: Do I believe that I am not just a carbon copy of any other pitcher?

Date	Answer

Mental Perspective

Pitching And Timidity

Pitching is not for the timid. The art of pitching requires that I be imaginative. It also requires that I have a sense of dimension and the ability to command a panoramic view of the inner and outer zone. I cannot be a creature of convention and relegate myself to pitching within the zone. If my dimension is so limited, my objective may never be achieved.

To become an effective pitcher, I must be like the child who colors outside the lines in a coloring book. I might think that this will be an easy task as every child has done it. This, however, is simply not so.

I must be a master of detail outside the established lines – an outlaw, a renegade, a loner, a nonconformist. To be sure – a visionary. I am confident that the picture I color outside the lines is most beautiful and pleasing.

Living this way requires patience and discipline so that my expertise may be developed. In order to cultivate this expertise, I must take a holistic view of the zone that exists outside the established strike zone. With this view vividly etched in my very existence, I must then be able to touch this zone by way of my pitch selections.

The remarkable and unduplicable beauty of pitching is that I experience this art's wildness and freedom. My lifestyle on the mound must be anything but orthodox. I must be able to see what is on the outside and on the inside at the same time. I am fearless and willing to throw any pitch at any time. I refuse to be a meek and narrow-minded drone who lives life devoid of vitality. As a pitcher, nothing can be, or is, the same.

Nothing can be what it appears to be unless the particular pitch I throw will have the desired effect of fooling the batter. If my pitches are packaged neatly and predictably, my life on the mound will be short. I will then find myself in green pastures outside the white lines.

A batter can be duped for only so long by a pitcher with the same dull and unvaried offerings. If something seemingly different is offered each time, my chances of longevity improve immeasurably.

My mission as a pitcher is to offer the batter the world, but give him nothing. My pitch should be wrapped and presented so that it is irresistible, Sirenic, and illusory. The batter wants it, covets it, and has to have it either because it is the perfect pitch for him or he is mesmerized by its enchanting allure. The batter cannot control himself.

Temptation must become one of my strongest traits. Seduction, my trademark. Chicanery, an insatiable passion. Deceptive, my indelible moniker.

Pausing and reflecting momentarily, the game of baseball is so steeped in tradition and goodness that it appears oddly contradictory that the most effective pitchers are those who are not constrained by the inherent characteristics of the game. Rather, the pitcher who is an outsider is revered and rewarded for his nonconformism. A pitcher who learns to live this way will be unable to live any other way.

It is urged that a higher and expansive consciousness be adopted in order to have more fun and be more effective in a long life on the mound. The true pitcher will find this life more stimulating, daring, provocative and immensely satisfying. As a pitcher, following each outing I will leave the field knowing that I have lived my life to the fullest based upon my ingenuity. Heaven really is on earth. Or, at the least, heaven is on the mound.

In coming of pitching age, be profligate and unrestrained. Strike out in all directions and locations with pitches. Be seemingly varied and unpredictable.

The life of a pitcher is not worth living if it is on a straight line through the established zone of the known. There is nothing less enjoyable in life than scripted monotony.

I must let my imagination run wild. The world, and the mound, are mine. I am the master of my destiny.

I inhabit the inside as well as the outside universe of the established black and white zonal world of the plate. I am hell-bent on achieving my mark – not hesitant. I am tenacious and not tentative.

Pitching, and life, are not for the timid. I shall step forward and explore the new and real world!

My Coach

QUESTION: Do I ever feel that my coach does not like me as much as the other players and does not have confidence in my abilities to play the game?

Date	Answer

QUESTION: If the answer to the previous question was "yes," is there any particular frequency that I feel this way?

Date	Answer

QUESTION: If the answer to the previous question was "yes," why have I felt that the coach does not like me as much as the other players?

Date	Answer

QUESTION: If I have felt this way, is it wrong to feel this way?

Date	Answer

QUESTION: What does this feeling mean?

Date	Answer

QUESTION: How do I resolve this feeling?

Date	Answer

QUESTION: Am I willing to discuss with my coaches the things that bother me or interfere with my playing the game of baseball?

Date	Answer

QUESTION: It is a game day. I arrive at the field in my uniform and I do not know who is pitching the game. I begin my warm up and am approximately one hour into my warm up routine and I still do not know who is pitching. My coach comes up to me and says: "John is just getting his spikes on. I was going to start him, but he is late so I guess we will have to go with you today."
How do I think and feel?

Date	Answer

QUESTION: I am under 5'10" and my fastball is below 80 mph on the gun. At the first team meeting my coach states that he is looking for pitchers who are over 5'10" and can throw at least 82 mph. He further tells my team that any pitcher who does not meet these basic qualifications does not have a chance either as a college player or as a professional. How do I personally deal with what my coach has said? How should I resolve what he has said if I plan to continue playing baseball?

Date	Answer

QUESTION: My coach tells me that there are other players on the team who are really the stars and I should look up to them as examples. He seems to focus his attention on those players and not me regardless of whether I am considered to be a good player. My coach really lights up when he talks about those other players. How do I deal with this behavior on the part of my coach?

Date	Answer

QUESTION: As a pitcher, I like to call my own pitches. However, either the coach or the catcher calls the pitches in each game and I am not permitted to shake-off a pitch no matter what pitch I believe is a better pitch to throw. How do I work with the coach or the catcher and not have on my mind the pitch that I want to throw or believe is the best pitch to throw at that time?

Date	Answer

QUESTION: How do I deal with several coaches giving me differing instruction on pitching?

Date	Answer

Mental Perspective

DIFFERENT COACHES GIVING DIFFERING INSTRUCTION ON PITCHING

- There is something to learn in everything I see, hear, or do.
- Always listen to what is being said rather than who is saying it.
- Read and study everything I can on pitching so that I will be educated and, thus, able to make proper choices.
- Videotape and review my pitching.
- Always communicate with my coaches, use reason, and do not be afraid to troubleshoot.
- Ask questions.
- When met with conflicting opinions by different coaches, always choose the method that is mechanically correct so that I can pitch forever.
- Do not be afraid to try something new – it may work for me.
- Learning a more effective way takes dedication and practice.
- I love this game and nothing is going to stand in the way of my playing it.

QUESTION: Am I committed to myself, my team, and to the game of baseball?

Date	Answer

Notes To Myself

Fourth Inning

Game Day

QUESTION: What gets me up for a game?

Date	Answer

QUESTION: During the game, what motivates me?

Date	Answer

QUESTION: Describe my mental and physical preparation on a game day when I know I will be pitching.

Date	Answer

QUESTION: Describe my mental and physical preparation on a game day when I know I will not be pitching.

Date	Answer

QUESTION: Describe my mental and physical preparation on a game day and I am pitching against the league-leading team with nine very good hitters in the lineup.

Date	Answer

QUESTION: Describe my mental and physical preparation on a game day and I am pitching against the team with the worst record in the league.

Date	Answer

QUESTION: Describe my mental and physical preparation on a game day and I know I will not be pitching, but I will be in the lineup.

Date	Answer

QUESTION: Describe my mental and physical preparation on the next day when I have back-to-back games and I pitched the day before.

Date	Answer

QUESTION: Describe my mental and physical preparation in the second game of a doubleheader and I pitched the first game.

Date	Answer

QUESTION: Describe my mental and physical preparation on a game day and I will not play because I am injured.

Date	Answer

QUESTION: Describe my mental and physical preparation on a practice day.

Date	Answer

QUESTION: In reviewing all of my answers to the previous questions in this chapter, what have I learned?

Date	Answer

QUESTION: What should I have learned?

Date	Answer

QUESTION: I am the starting pitcher on game day and have completed my pre-game warm up. It is game time and the game is delayed for at least one hour for whatever reason I can imagine. How, historically, has this affected me mentally and physically on being told of a game delay?

Date	Answer

QUESTION: Same scenario as the previous question. How should I be affected mentally and physically on being told of the game delay?

Date	Answer

QUESTION: Same scenario as the two previous questions. What can I do to avoid being physically and mentally overcome by a game delay?

Date	Answer

Mental Perspective

Preparedness

A pitcher is always ready to pitch, no matter what – at least, mentally!

Notes To Myself

FIFTH INNING

Having Fun And Playing Baseball

QUESTION: In the context of being a baseball player, what does it mean that: "I just want to have fun playing baseball?"

Date	Answer

QUESTION: What are the ingredients of "having fun?"

Date	Answer

QUESTION: Is wanting to have fun sometimes an excuse or justification for something else? If so, please explain.

Date	Answer

QUESTION: Have I ever quit doing something because I said I was not having fun?

Date	Answer

QUESTION: If I quit doing something because I said I was not having fun, did I really quit because I had a fear of failure or I did not want to work hard enough to achieve success?

Date	Answer

Mental Perspective

METHOD

According to Webster's Third New International Dictionary (1993), method is defined as ". . . a way, technique or process of or for doing something . . ."

Being An Effective Pitcher – And Having Fun At The Same Time

- I feel good about myself.
- I feel good about my life.
- I am physically sound.
- I am mechanically sound.
- I feel good about my pre-game preparation.
- I can, and shall, throw any pitch called and I can place it anywhere I want.
- I feel relaxed and not rushed, but I still have the butterflies going in my stomach.
- I am uncomplicated by persons and things around me.
- I love this game and nothing is going to stand in the way of my playing it.
- I am good enough to be on this baseball field.
- I let my unconscious take over.

QUESTION: If I get out of my mind who is calling my pitches and what is being called, will I be a more effective pitcher?

Date	Answer

QUESTION: If my answer to the previous question was "yes," please explain.

Date	Answer

QUESTION: If my answer to the question was "no," please explain.

Date	Answer

QUESTION: Should I ever question a pitch called by the umpire?

Date	Answer

QUESTION: If my answer to the previous question was "yes," please explain.

Date	Answer

QUESTION: If my answer was "no," please explain.

Date	Answer

List the reasons why, historically, I have lost concentration in a game.

Date	Answer

QUESTION: It is either a practice day or a game day. I am at the field long before the appointed time. Earlier that day my girlfriend broke up with me and I had no prior notice. I thought everything was going just fine. I was devastated. Whether this has ever happened to me, how might I be thinking and feeling at the game or practice?

Date	Answer

QUESTION: Same scenario as previous question. How should I be thinking and feeling?

Date	Answer

QUESTION: Same scenario as previous questions. What am I going to do to make certain that I play effectively that day?

Date	Answer

QUESTION: Same scenario as previous questions. How am I going to achieve my objective of playing effectively that day?

Date	Answer

Notes To Myself

Sixth Inning

Mental Perspective
Breathing Life Into Myself
A Technique Of Breathing

- As I inhale, my diaphragm expands.

- As I exhale, my diaphragm contracts.

- As I breathe, I do so through both my nose and my mouth.

- I concentrate on the act of breathing itself with eyes open or closed depending upon what works for me.

- My mental sense at all times is that: Things will always work out no matter what.

- My breathing pattern is consistent, but the pace may increase or decrease depending upon my particular situation or stress level.

- I do not let into my mind or think of anything else while breathing. My focus is fixed.

- If the situation does not permit the total blocking out of everything around me, then I, at least, use the regulated act of breathing itself to calm me down. My goal is to achieve total mind and body relaxation from head to foot.

- I take ten slow breaths before I go to the mound each inning and after I have returned at the end of the inning.

- I use proper breathing technique at all times on the mound and whether I am striking everybody out or giving up monster home runs.

QUESTION: Why is proper breathing technique important?

Date	Answer

Notes To Myself

Notes To Myself

SEVENTH INNING

Personal Evaluation

In no more than 25 words, evaluate my life in baseball thus far.

Date	Answer

QUESTION: How many days per week, and for how long in my life, do I want to play baseball?

Date	Answer

QUESTION: In answering the previous question, what was the first thought that came into my mind?

Date	Answer

QUESTION: What was the second thought that came into my mind?

Date	Answer

QUESTION: Am I giving myself mixed messages?

Date	Answer

QUESTION: Is baseball the most important thing to me in my life?

Date	Answer

QUESTION: If baseball is not the most important thing to me in my life, please explain.

Date	Answer

QUESTION: How will the answer "yes" or "no" to the two previous questions affect me on the field?

Date	Answer

QUESTION: Should the answer to these questions affect me on the field?

Date	Answer

QUESTION: Whether baseball is the most important thing in my life, what should I do?

Date	Answer

QUESTION: Presently, what things about my life make me the most confident?

Date	Answer

QUESTION: Presently, what are the worst fears I have about myself as a person?

Date	Answer

QUESTION: Presently, in what areas am I the most confident as a pitcher?

Date	Answer

QUESTION: As a pitcher, what are the worst fears I have about myself?

Date	Answer

QUESTION: Do I believe I can play baseball for the rest of my life?

Date	Answer

QUESTION: Do I want to play baseball for the rest of my life?

Date	Answer

Mental Perspective

STICKING WITH IT

There are a lot of things going on in my life that I may understand, do not understand, or really do not notice. However, things are beginning to tug at me. I am becoming more aware of myself and others. Maybe I am even becoming self-conscious.

I am beginning to awaken to life – friends; the opposite sex; parental pressure; parties; a desire to do what I want and not be told what to do; I want to be cool; I want to be accepted; I may have even considered or become involved in activities that are considered to be socially unacceptable or even illegal. In short, I am being assaulted by pressure after pressure and it is unrelenting. Who am I? What am I? Where am I? Where am I going? What do I want to do? With whom do I want to do it?

QUESTION: How do I deal with my unfolding life and not lose interest in and still have the time to play baseball?

Date	Answer

Notes To Myself

Notes To Myself

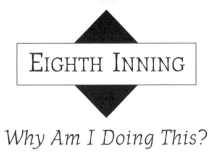

EIGHTH INNING

Why Am I Doing This?

QUESTION: As a pitcher, what are my goals this coming year and in my life as a pitcher?

Date	Answer

QUESTION: How am I going to specifically achieve my goals this year and in my life as a pitcher?

Date	Answer

QUESTION: How will I be able to measure whether I have achieved these goals?

Date	Answer

QUESTION: How often should I measure my progress toward achieving my goals?

Date	Answer

Mental Perspective

EFFECTIVE

According to Webster's Third New International Dictionary (1993), effective is defined as ". . . marked by the quality of being influential or exerting positive influence . . . able to accomplish a purpose . . ."

I love this game and nothing is going to stand in the way of my playing it. As a pitcher, what is my purpose?

Notes To Myself

Ninth Inning

Here's The Pitch – A Method
The Dime

We are in the ninth, and final, inning. There are few precious moments left. Chances are that a diverse group has read this book: pitchers, parents, relatives, friends of pitchers, and coaches. So, to close out on the same page, I have selected a topic all of us have in common.

Let's talk about money. After all, doesn't money have its hand in all of our pockets so to speak? Doesn't it?

Don't get me wrong, though. I am not here to lecture on financial planning. I am not here to cause you to get the big and small picture on money.

More specifically, let's talk about one thin dime. The question for us to consider is: What does the dime have to do with effective pitching?

There are two parts to the answer. First, what is on the dime? Second, what is in the dime?

What Is On The Dime?
Seeing the Dime

The dime is a very small object. All of us can picture the dime, however, in order to see a dime we must narrow our focus or it will be lost in the larger landscape.

As a pitcher, you must be able to put your pitches on the dime or you will not be on the mound. Your focus is narrow. Your goal is narrow. Your dime is located in a different place depending upon the pitch called and its location. You need not rely upon home plate, the catcher's mitt, or any variable part of the batter's or catcher's anatomy. The singularity of the dime is your constant target. The dime is the destination point of each pitch. If you can see the dime, then you can place your pitch on the dime. The dime beckons.

Thus, I ask you to get the small picture of pitching and not the big picture. Simplify this great art by reading the small print in a manner of speaking. If you are going to place your pitch on the dime, you have no time to be distracted by the larger world around you. Your gaze is fixed to the matter at-hand.

There are no longer any outside temptations to doing your duty. Your duty is to get batters out. There are no exceptions to this duty. Anything that shifts your focus from doing your duty stands in the way of getting batters out and must be disregarded. This means anything! Any broader outlook will prove disastrous as you must be single-minded.

Ralph Waldo Emerson urged us to "Hitch your wagon to a star." His message is very visual. In it you see a road map to success. The dime is no different. You have your eyes on it every pitch of the way toward success; that being, to becoming an effective pitcher.

Feeling the Dime

Close your eyes and imagine the feel of a dime. Place it between your thumb and index finger. It is very small and smooth. It is comforting to rub it. You may even think it has a charm-like quality to it.

As a pitcher, you must be able to feel the ball and its destination on the dime. It is very comforting indeed!

But, you may ask, "How do I get my pitches on the dime?" If you have been a serious student of this book, you have discovered by now that the dime is an acronym for determination, ingenuity, method, and effectiveness. What is on the dime are your pitches. Now, let us look to see what is in the dime.

What Is In The Dime?

Look to the spelling of dime. In it you have an "i" and a "me." That's right – you! And nobody else but you! You are the only one who can make yourself a person and a pitcher. Ultimately, you are the only one on the mound. Sound lonely? Absolutely not. Sound challenging? Absolutely!

Your determination is in the dime. Your ingenuity is in the dime. Your method of learning to pitch is in the dime. As a result, your effectiveness as a pitcher is in the dime.

Ultimate Mental Perspective

For as little as a dime, then, are you willing to invest in yourself? Don't let anything stand in the way of your playing this game. And, always ask yourself: "In whom must I trust?"

About The Author

Jim Lopez is an attorney practicing law for the past twenty years in Tacoma, Washington. He is a member of the law firm of Lowenberg, Lopez & Hansen, P.S.

His childhood dream was to be a pitcher in the majors. He played through high school and semi-professional after college. Through the years, his reality has been the enjoyment of two most noble professions; those being, teaching and the law. But, he has never forgotten how to pitch and how to coach.

Jim is 49 years of age and is a pitcher in an over-30 men's baseball league in Tacoma. Since 1990, he has played in the Roy Hobbs World Series in Fort Myers, Florida and the Men's Senior Baseball League World Series in Phoenix, Arizona.

For the past four years, Jim has been the pitching coach for the Puyallup High School baseball team in Puyallup, Washington. The team has been ranked in the top ten in Washington for the past three years.

He is currently in the process of completing a book about over-30 baseball entitled *The Promise of Spring*.